Lessons from My Grandmother's Lap

An Anthology Compiled by
Regina "Sunshine" Robinson

Copyright © 2018 by Regina Robinson

Published by the Leading Through Living Community, LLC

All rights reserved. Scripture quotations are from the Holy Bible, King James Version (KJV) - www.Bible.com

All Rights Reserved. No part or portion of this publication may be reproduced, stored in a retrieval system, or transmitted in any form or by any means - electronic, mechanical, photocopying, recording, or otherwise - without the express written consent of the author.

For information:
Leading Through Living Community LLC
6790 W. Broad Street Suite 300
Douglasville, GA 30134

ISBN-13: 978-0989145718

DEDICATION

When my Grandma Snook passed, it was the first time in my life I was without a grandparent. I was fortunate to have four grandparents who were a part of my life. I am blessed.

To Granddaddy Sidney Gore Sr. and Grandma Patsy Gore: thank you for the time spent and shared. Although I wasn't your biological grandchild, your door was always open to me.

To my Granddaddy James Alford Sr., who was the first man to love me: thank you for showing me what it looks like when a man loves and provides for his family.

To Grandma Snook, Elizabeth Allen Alford for always closing the gaps in my life and loving me so completely. Your example makes me want to be the best grandma ever because every child deserves to have a grandma like you.

So although my Grandma Snook inspired this book, I want to dedicate this book to all of my grandparents and to every grandmother on these pages. May their examples and their spirits live on in the way we love others.

CONTENTS

	Introduction	i
1	A Heart to Give	1
2	It's Hard, But It's Fair and Even A Fool Can Tell You Something	9
3	Washing Dishes: A Practical Lesson	17
4	The Inner Strength of A Grand Lioness	23
5	The Proverbs of Grandma Lena	31
6	Abundant Love	39
7	Royal Queen	47
8	About the Business of Love	55
9	Sacrifice in Love	61
10	Wear Your Fur… Even in the Summer	69
11	Mama's Sweet Bread	77
12	My Personal Vessels of Agape Love	85
	GrandMa	93

INTRODUCTION

My earliest memories of my Grandmother are of us praying together. We would be on our knees on the side of her bed, eyes closed, and our hands folded in prayer. It's how she always prayed, and I mimicked her every step. She would start to pray and would pray for everyone I could remember knowing in my life. She prayed up one side of the street and back down the other side. She covered her entire neighborhood in prayer. She prayed for what seemed like hours to a young mind. Her words were part conversation and part worship. Through the eyes and ears of a child, it felt like I was privileged to sit at the feet of God and hear intimate conversations between Him and His favorite daughter. Afterward, Grandmother would put me in bed and under the heaviest quilts known to man. LOL.

My grandparents' home was my safe space. The place where love was abundant, and God was real. Those memories are special to me and they are at the core of how I formed my relationship with the Father.

When I think of my Grandmother, these are some of the first memories that pop up. I've shared this memory of her with audiences all over this country as I have traveled and shared with audiences large and small, professional and personable. I've heard so many times how people have been blessed by my stories about my grandmother. So after she passed away, I began looking for ways to keep her memory and lessons alive.

I've always known that I would write about her. I began sharing the prospect of writing about her and the response was more than I expected. Not only were those around me excited, they began to tell me about their grandmothers. I found that there were so many people eager to share the powerful impact their grandmothers made on them and the world.

This book is the result of a small group of us opening our hearts and sharing these amazing women with the world. I can't wait for you to meet all the women in this book and experience their voices. You will be blessed. You will be changed. More than anything, I hope you are inspired to share your grandmother with us. There's one thing I know for sure: our grandmothers may be gone from the physical realm, but their spirits and their lessons live forever.

An Anthology Compiled by REGINA "SUNSHINE" ROBINSON

Be blessed, changed, and inspired

CHAPTER ONE
A HEART TO GIVE

Her Story: Elizabeth Allen Alford

The world knew her as Elizabeth Allen Alford. To me, she was Grandma Snook. She was the biggest lover and giver that I had ever known. I saw her sow into God's Kingdom and into the lives of others in such a natural and beautiful way that giving became a way of life for me.

Grandma shared with me that people often asked her how her and my granddaddy, James Alford, Sr., were able to do so much with (what may have seemed to others) so little while other people seemed to struggle. She would tell them that too many people don't have anything because "their fist is closed". My grandmother would hold up her fist to demonstrate this to me. Grandma Snook explained that people received blessings, and then they closed their hands around that blessing to try to hold on to it. She would then open her hand wide and explain the real secret was to open your hands and give it away. Then God would bless you even more. Over the course of her life, I would hear that story repeatedly. Her words forever echo in my mind.

I thought everyone gave because it's what I knew and saw her do. In fact, she would look for ways to give. If she knew someone needed help, she would create jobs for them to perform so that she could bless them. Something as simple as changing the batteries in her remote or tightening the toilet seat might warrant a pay of $20-40. She was so creative in her giving. And although people knew what she was doing, they were blessed in the way that she honored their dignity.

My grandma not only gave money, she gave things she knew people needed. From buying clothes for a family to providing groceries, I have seen her do it all. Giving was one of the biggest joys of her life. She was a giving Mastermind. Grandma Snook would pay attention to everything you said and did so that she could hear a need and meet it.

She was the same way with gift giving. Multiple times in my life, I would come home to my parent's house to find presents on my bed that had been left by her. Once I was out shopping for church dresses with her. While looking, I paused to admire a long acid-wash blue jean coat. Yeah, I said, "Acid wash." I loved it, but when I saw the price tag, I put it back. Grandma never said a word or even gave any indication that she saw me with the coat. About a week later, I came home from school to find a big white box on my bed. It was that coat. WOW! I was in tears. It was one of those moments that you never forget. From that point forward, I was a little careful not to linger too long looking at anything because I knew she was watching and I didn't want her to spend all her money on me.

One thing she was also known for was knowing everyone's favorite dish or dessert, and having that dish when you went to her house. But not just that; there was also a dish set aside for you to take home as well. Let me tell you what I mean. When Thanksgiving rolled around, she worked hard to prepare her signature dishes: ham, potato salad, banana pudding, chicken salad, and I can't leave off that sweet potato bread. Ummm hmmmm. She cooked a lot of things, but these are things you were guaranteed to find at every big family meal. And if she found out that something was your favorite and it wasn't already a part of the menu, it was added. Then once you were leaving to go home, she would call you to the side and give you your own personal dish of your favorite item to take home.

When my husband, John, started going home with me to visit, he had a piece of REAL lemon pound cake at my grandmother's house. He commented on how good it was, and of course, she sent some home with him. Now, this cake wasn't baked by my grandma, but by a close family friend, Ms. Lucille Thomas. Grandma would get a lemon pound cake from her from time to time. Well, from that day forward, anytime she knew John was coming, she had Ms. Lucille make a cake. Not only that though. From our next visit after John's REAL lemon pound cake experience, until her health failed where she could no longer provide, my grandmother would have a lemon pound cake just for John to take back home with him. But guess what: she would also have a pan of my favorite - banana pudding - for me, AND would have a plate of ham that could feed a whole family just for my son, Gabe. Yeah, Gabe loves meat! Grandma Snook was the Queen of making everyone feel special, and like each person was her favorite.

My Grandma also believed in giving her time. She served on a level I still haven't experienced after her. As a senior citizen with a cane, she would still go to the homes of other elderly people and clean for them, cook for them, and just be their friend. She would take them to doctor's appointments and to the grocery store. She would always say, "Grandma can't sit still baby. I get stiff." Any excuse was a good excuse to help others.

But the most powerful example I saw was her commitment to the Kingdom. I learned to tithe from her. It was the cornerstone of all her giving. Even when she was on a limited, fixed income and my mother Geraldine Gore and my sister Pamelia Stanley helped her with her bills, she would say, "I gotta pay my tithes." With my grandma, God was always first. That's where the root of her giving heart came from. You hear people say all the time, "You can't beat God giving." Well, my grandma sure seemed like she was making a good run at trying.

An Anthology Compiled by REGINA "SUNSHINE" ROBINSON

My Lesson

From watching my Grandma Snook, here is what I know for sure. Giving is the real joy of life. If we make the commitment to give to God's Kingdom and to His children, every day in our lives will be filled with joy. I saw this walked out before me. So I'm not telling you something I heard. I'm telling you what I know.

"Give, and it will be given to you: good measure, pressed down, shaken together, and running over will be put into your bosom. For with the same measure that you use, it will be measured back to you."
Luke 6:38 New King James Version (NKJV)

Regina Sunshine Robinson is an Author, Motivational Speaker, Talk Show Host, Empowerment Coach, Corporate Trainer, and Teacher. She is CEO of Regina Sunshine Global Network, parent company to everything Regina Sunshine including EWATE, a Women's Empowerment Organization whose main purpose is to empower and encourage women to be all they were created to be in order to fulfill God's perfect plan for their lives. Their slogan is "We'll Help You Get Your SASSY Back." Tune in to Regina's acclaimed talk show "The Regina Sunshine Show" on Comcast 24 People TV Tuesdays at 12 pm EST and on Regina Sunshine Global Network Mondays at 7 pm EST to get a weekly dose of her Regina Sunshine State of Mind. Regina Sunshine is also the Editor in Chief of *BOLD Plus Magazine*. Regina's personal motto is "It's Not Over Til I Win" and she wins when she sees others "WINNING". For more information, to book her or to follow her on Social Media, go to ReginaSunshine.com.

An Anthology Compiled by REGINA "SUNSHINE" ROBINSON

The secret to getting more blessings: open your hands and give them away

CHAPTER TWO
IT'S HARD, BUT IT'S FAIR, AND EVEN A FOOL CAN TELL YOU SOMETHING

Her Story: *Viola Rebecca Mathis*

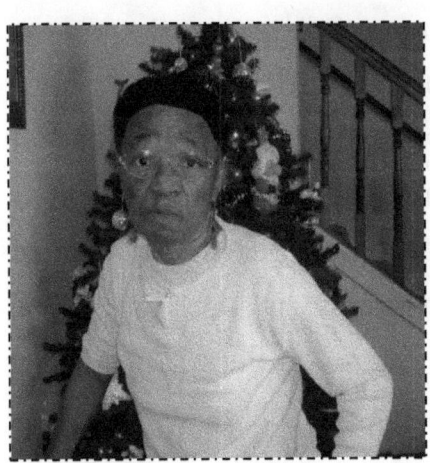

My grandmother Viola Rebecca Mathis was a pistol! Ask anyone. They'll tell you. Beck (or Becky Lee, as she was affectionately called) was known for her feisty nature and unwillingness to tolerate BS. She always had a quick comeback and could not be corrected when it came to certain things.

She was a cook. She worked at the pepper plant. She ran a boarding home. She raised five children, seven grandchildren and cared for several others who were not related to her. She was an unincorporated bail bondsman. She had street credibility. People knew not to mess with her. People also knew they could come to her in their time of need. She was not your average grandmama!

My Lesson

I'm not sure when it happened, but one day I opened my mouth and my grandmama came out. People would say, "You sound just like your grandmama", except they had never even met her before. Particularly after her passing, I'd find myself recalling and using phrases I had not heard since I was a child. Never intentionally, it just happened. Oh, it seems the sayings were endless, and I can hear them now:

> *"Baby got to crawl before he can walk."*
>
> *"I done forgot more than you'll ever learn."*

"The first hen to cackle is the one that laid the egg."

"I'm gone get you for old and new."

"I can show you better than I can tell you."

Oh, there were so many phrases that annoyed me at the time. Why couldn't she just say what she was saying? But now these sayings have proved to be my source of wisdom and comfort in some of life's most challenging situations.

It's hard, but it's fair. It took a long time for this saying to catch up to me. I mean, I heard it; but I didn't *hear* it. I just thought it was something my grandmama said when something got a little tough and she didn't have the means to do anything about it. Was I ever wrong! Think about it. A situation is considered fair when all parties involved benefit in some way, right? How can something be hard and fair at the same time? It's all about perspective. It is often said that anything worth having is worth working hard for. I think this is what my grandmama was trying to get us to understand. She wanted us to know that although there may have been some struggle, it would always be worth it in the end. There was always something good that could come out of anything if we chose to see it.

It's hard, but it's fair. My lupus… It's definitely hard, but it's fair too. Were it not for my illness requiring me to resign from my teaching job, I would not be living my ideal life. It is hard, but it also fair! This is a pretty extreme example, but I don't want this point to be lost upon you as it was with me for so many years.

Recognizing that it's hard, but it's fair can completely change the way that you approach difficult situations. If you go into them knowing that you will come out of them with something that you did not have before, wouldn't your entire attitude change? How many times have you not wanted to do something, if it weren't for (fill in the blank)? Just knowing that you'd get something out of the experience gave you at least enough fortitude to move forward. It's hard, but it's fair.

Coming from a person who didn't like to be corrected, it was ironic that I often heard my grandmama say, *"Even a fool can tell you something."* She usually said this in response to one of us kids telling the others to "shut up", *"you'n know what you talkin' 'bout'* or *"you'n tell me what to do"*. She made it clear that we all had something to contribute. I'm sure we didn't see it that way at the time. No, at the time, we figured that one of us was being a labeled a fool and that my Beck was just trying to make sure that the fool didn't feel left out.

Looking back on all my experiences as a teenager, young adult, and now mature woman, "Even a fool can tell you something," has to be the most valuable lesson that I learned from my grandmama. This phrase taught me to look for the lesson in everything and to find value in the words spoken by those with whom I may not agree or even like. This has served me well in my personal life and in business. You see, this has helped me to think more rationally about things rather than leading with my emotions. I've learned to think objectively when it comes to certain things. No one is all wrong or all right all of the time. In fact, "Everybody ain't gone tell the same lie," according to my grandmama; so I now understand that even the most unpopular opinions hold some weight and should be considered.

For her, I don't think it was that deep. To a degree,

yes, there were lessons to be taught, but overall, she was just being herself sharing what she called, "motherwit". She knew that one day her words would serve us well. She used to always say, "Keep livin'."

What really stands out to me is that my grandmama and I were not extremely close. Of course I thought we were when I was child. That was until I realized she was close to all us grandkids in different ways. She'd tell me that I had cousins who had all types of PhDs and degrees, but then when I mentioned enrolling in a doctoral program she informed me that if I wasn't writing "'scriptions", I would not be a doctor. It was just her way and I appreciate it. After all, it's hard, but it's fair and even a fool can tell you something!

Dr. Marquita S. Blades is an award-winning Educator, international speaker, author, and education consultant with 16 years of experience as a high school science teacher and manager of national STEM programs for high-achieving high school students. Dr. Blades is currently a full-time Education Consultant, the owner of Dr. Blades Consulting, and the host of The Dr. Marquita Blades Show: Candid Conversations that Create Change, a radio show dedicated to discussing current trends and issues in education. Dr. Blades' Consulting firm offers solutions to learning institutions and individuals through professional development programs, curriculum and assessment development, and conference development and programming services. Dr. Blades is also the founder of The Mediocre Teacher Project© which helps other teachers avoid and battle through burnout by incorporating their unique gifts and talents into their daily practice. When she is not working, Dr. Blades enjoys reading, cooking, and traveling with her husband. Learn more about Dr. Blades and her work by visiting www.drmarquitablades.com.

An Anthology Compiled by REGINA "SUNSHINE" ROBINSON

Even a fool can tell you something: no one is all wrong or all right all of the time

CHAPTER THREE
WASHING DISHES: A PRACTICAL LESSON

Her Story: Louise P. Moore

She was pure and sweet as Candy, which is what her peers called her. Her students at Huntington Park High School in Los Angeles called her Mrs. Moore. I just called her Grand Mommie. She was elegant and firm, disciplined and dedicated, secretive, and my source of life.

I remember being just a shoulder above the kitchen sink when the lesson began. Kitchen duty was washing dishes after eating those "oh so good for you" meals. Without fail, I cleaned my plate (except for the greens, I did not like greens)! No collards, or turnips, oh no, not me! I would ball them up, and into the trash they would go. I am sure she knew, but never said a word; she let me think I was smart and could outwit her.

I remember washing dishes by hand and feeling the food float around like waves of seaweed and sand. "Nasty," I would say to myself while frowning and pouting. Grand Mommie spotted my face with the look of disgrace and in her genius, she then taught me to scrape the plate. Into the trash first so my hands would not feel so bad. The water was oh so hot that my fingers would wrinkle and I would get red spots. It saddened me when the bubbles would disappear and the water was left a color other than clear. I would empty the tub the dishes were in and fill it up again and again. See, she taught me to run my fingers across each plate, around and around, I would have to touch every place. If I felt anything, back in the water it would go, using the dishrag to remove every particle. I repeated this time and time again, it was something I rushed because I wanted to be finished and have this particular chore end. I wanted to be quick with it, get it done, go watch TV and have some fun. I wanted to play my way with my dolls and stuff. I did not care that I always rushed.

But one night Grand Mommie had enough; she found food on some dishes because I rushed. She told me to wash those dishes again, and if it happened another time, well you know I would get a whip'n. But most of all, I would have to wash every dish in the entire kitchen. I am sure you can guess that it happened again, and I am still not sure what time she woke me for my promised discipline. With tears in my eyes, and to no surprise, the counter next to the sink was sky high. Every plate, cup, saucer, pot and pan ready to be washed over again. "Oh no, it's so many," as I thought to myself, "There's not even one left on the shelf." I was perplexed and ashamed that I did not do it right. I had failed and with no one to blame. My face puffed up and my tears remained. I could not hide them, not even one. Even if it took until the morning sun, all the dishes had to get done. I know my tears had to rinse a few and I knew not to complain due to my fear, but in the end, the kitchen was clean, the counter clear, and every dish dried and put away like my last tear.

I do not recall going back to sleep that night as I may have had the fright of my life. However, even today when I wash the dishes by hand and my wrinkled fingers rub across a plate or swirl my sponge inside a glass, I take the time to be careful and patient, all because of that one night. With time, we learned it is more practical to do something correctly once than to do something incorrectly and carelessly while feeling like a dunce. Therefore, the next time you have a chore to do, be practical, be patient; it is all up to you.

My Lesson

There would be no master degree, no home, no business, and most of all no love for myself for doing better in life as it only follows being better. Having patience with myself and doing things right the first time (if possible) save me from unnecessary stress and anxiety. I have grown into a positive and "extra" ordinary woman because I honor the lesson of having practical patience. It is with ultimate respect and my deepest of gratitude to honor the memory of Louise P. Moore as I live out this lesson from my grandmother's lap.

Angelina Hunt, MS received her Master's degree from Springfield College and completed her Life Coach Certification at Southwest Institute of Healing Arts. She offers comprehensive coaching and mentor services to young adult and adult leaders. Angelina professional background includes higher education, Non-profits, and Human Services organizations. Her gifts are to support and coach individuals through life's difficult disappointments through the areas of personal growth, parenting, and self-love. She has assisted clients with depression, self-esteem, goal setting and unique life concerns that hinder personal evolution and success. Additionally, she has a special love interest in working with women to encourage them to dream a bigger dream by developing motivational strategies to explore their life's passion. Her approach integrates positive psychology, community psychology and the law of love and attraction, to develop lifelong changes that enhance and empower the soul, heart and mind. Contact Angelina on Facebook and Instagram Facebook: @aatheart, and on her website at www.aatheart.com.

Lessons from My Grandmother's Lap

CHAPTER FOUR
THE INNER STRENGTH OF A GRAND LIONESS

Her Story: Miriam Reid

"Where there is no struggle, there is no strength."
-*Oprah Winfrey*
https://www.brainyquote.com/quotes/oprah_winfrey_133739?src=t_strength

At the age of three, I was dropped off in Ms. Miriam Reid's care and protection. I thought it was temporary, since I was in the care of ever-changing faces of family.

When we initially met, I remembered Ms. Reid's piercing gaze that had a great deal to say, but very little to give financially. Yet she accepted me, and my brothers who came years later, with an open heart of love and humility.

She toiled in the heart-drenched sun daily with sweat dripping down her face. It nourished the foundation of love and security which she used to raise us. She was always on the go, and barely took the time to sit and relax. I thought *nothing beats the clock like this hard-working woman of God*. In her own eyes, Ms. Reid was fulfilling her purpose in ensuring we were properly cared for, even until this day. I wondered at times, *where is this source of strength coming from?* Only to discover that they were divine manifestations from the grace of struggles she endured over the years.

Even though we were economically poor and disadvantaged, we were rich in hope and spirit. Ms. Reid managed to maintain herself and her cubs in times of unforeseen circumstances. In addition, her grand hands were riddled with fine lines of perseverance, apparent from her hard work to financially and emotionally sustain us. It was also noticeable in the worn-out house frock fading away by the many cycles of hand-washes, as well as the

5am to 8pm conductress uniform worn on the city bus daily.

Everyone depended on my grandmother, yet I wondered, *who does she depend on?* This woman of strength who often speaks with her eyes to the ground. Some days were still in silence, as she stared worriedly into the brick of space. Days of broken dreams from the struggles of a hard life to care for the little ones. I would imagine myself planting seed of words that whispered the lyrical tunes of Bob Marley singing, "Don't worry about a thing. Every little thing is going to be alright." This was my way to comfort her silent woos. In very little time though, she always regained her composure and allowed every negative experience to flow pass with no complaints, only in display of gratitude and kindness. "It worked!" I would say to God, not sure whether it was the song or her prayers. Undoubtedly, her faith was the light that propelled each way forward and upward. By listening to the words of God flowing within her, it was Ms. Reid's recourse to bounce back stronger and wiser than ever.

With each struggle that came along on her journey, my grandmother never ceased to show others love and compassion. Ms. Reid understood kindness through the vision of independence and mutual connectedness. She extended a welcoming hand to anyone in need of her service. She became a beacon of hope and inspiration for us to thrive in excellence and success for the future. For a woman of no words, Ms. Reid's best proclaimed words were, "Go to school and grow."

She never questioned us about our career goals. There was no, "What do you want to be?" or "Where do you want to go in life?" She already knew with her spiritual nurture that we would be able to discern our paths wisely on our own.

Ms. Reid's guiding wisdom and intuitive nature spoke through her assuring eyes. Every gaze emulated an inner strength and grace connecting the light of the Divine. Strength, wisdom, and understanding were only a few noticeable characteristics of this strong and virtuous lioness.

My Lesson

"Inner strength shines within the heart of every soul."

-Terry Shaw

There is a version of Ms. Reid in every one of us, waiting to surrender to our experiences. We have all had moments of struggles in our lives or times of diminishing confidence and courage, yet we continue to bounce back stronger than ever. Allow those trials to serve as an inspiration of your divine strength and faith within you. Allow each dark moment to be your teacher. As you grow from your experiences, allow inner strength, wisdom, and understanding to carry you through on your continuing journey. To truly embrace your lessons, you must simply allow every moment to flow in humility.

As I grasped my own inner strength on my journey, I can only begin to emulate the strength of my grandmother, this wonderful woman of God. Her nurturing grace and kindness served as a guiding light, even amid my own struggles. When I remember the words from my grandmother's eyes, I would rebound stronger knowing that the God within her lies within me. In every passing experience, I would be reminded of Ms. Reid's determination to never give up, only to see these lessons as emerging awareness of strength. I can now only begin to outpour the same unconditional love from my grandmother towards myself and others in this time and space reality.

An Anthology Compiled by REGINA "SUNSHINE" ROBINSON

In observing the ways of Ms. Reid, I can only continue to live with the sway of life's experiences. This helps me connect to the root of inner strength, which is the light of natural empowerment and virtue. I can only allow this light to flow from my heart as I move upwards on my journey. I duly embedded within my heart her lessons of love and strength. This is one of the most beautiful lessons of empowerment acquired from a graceful grand lioness.

Terry K. Shaw is the Business Specialist in the Mathematics and Computer Science Department at Rutgers University. She has a BA in Mathematics and MA in Economics from CUNY-Hunter College, where she held different  leadership roles for eight years. She is the Founder of Terry Shaw Inspires, which provides inspirational messages and spiritual advice to assist people in utilizing their own inner guide to thrive in love, success, and happiness. Born and raised in

Kingston, Jamaica, she enjoys reading poems, listening to Bob Marley's music, taking nature walks, and writing to inspire many others. She also serves as a Mentor in Big Brothers Big Sisters in Newark, NJ. You may email her at terrykshaw33@gmail.com or follow her on Facebook and Instagram at @terryshawinpires.

An Anthology Compiled by REGINA "SUNSHINE" ROBINSON

Trust that you are able to discern your own path, wisely and on your own

CHAPTER FIVE
THE PROVERBS OF GRANDMA LENA

Her Story: Lena Powell Wright

My grandmother, Lena Powell Wright, was perhaps the greatest influence of my life. Even though my grandmother was not afforded the luxury of a formal education, she was the wisest person I have ever known. A soft-spoken woman of few words, her presence commanded a high level of respect when she entered a room. She took everything seriously. In fact, I only heard her laugh twice in my life. She grew up during the Jim Crow era and began raising her family during the Great Depression. I remember her telling me of the pain she experienced when she first heard her own father, who she considered to be a superhero, be referred to as a boy by a white man, who was also a tobacco farmer. As a mother, she experienced what it is considered the greatest loss of having to bury three of her children as young adults. Those experiences birthed a wisdom that she passed on to her children.

The best way to describe her was lovingly stern. Her practical, no nonsense approach to life was larger than her four foot eleven stature.

My Lessons

Collins describes a proverb as an "enigmatic saying in which a profound truth is cloaked". My grandmother taught me so many lessons that continue to enrich my life and guide my experience as a woman. Even though I did not inherit her beautiful contralto voice, I am thankful that I was blessed with the lessons that she taught me. I call these lessons proverbs because while simple, they embody significant truths that I have taken with me across the globe.

It was in her lap and at her feet that I learned lessons that transcend time and space, and have comforted and guided me during the most difficult years of my life.

The Proverbs of Grandma Lena:
1. Always be kind to people. Not only does it feel good to do so, you never know who you will need later. A bit of kindness goes a long way, and being kind is free. It does not cost anything to show love and appreciation.

2. Hardworking people who trust God should never need an alarm clock. Have the task at hand on your mind before you go to bed and your body will wake up when it's supposed to.

In the eighteen years that I lived with my grandmother, I never saw her use an alarm or seem pressed for time. Whenever I would get stressed about having enough time to meet a deadline, she would say, "Relax, God is the creator of time."

3. Break a sweat every single day. Grandma Lena did not have a gym membership or work out goals. I remember her running with children in the neighborhood and playing hopscotch and jumping

rope in her seventies. Work your body!

4. Do not entertain gossip for one second. One day you may be the subject. Grandma Lena avoided all forms of gossip like the plague. And people knew that they could not do so in her presence.

5. Work hard all week, but do not work on Sundays. That is the day set aside for God and family. Following this piece of advice puts things into proper perspective. Now there is a tendency to always be plugged in with social media posts, loads of emails, and text messages. Avoid this.

6. It takes less effort to tell the truth. Make your life easier. Whatever your truth is, live it! Life is too hard to keep up with lies.

7. Prepare all of your clothes (wash, iron, sew) for the week on Saturday. It makes your weekday mornings much smoother. Even though I hated this as a child and thought it was tedious, Grandma Lena was giving me a valuable lesson in preparedness, and clearing your mind and space of clutter, which can interfere with your thinking.

8. Don't do anything half way. Giving less than 100 percent is worse than doing nothing at all. My

grandmother believed in giving your best at all times. If you cannot give your best when requested, then the answer should be a simple No. Giving less than your best is a disservice.

All of the children hated when Grandma oversaw an event at church because there would be no 'reading from the paper'. We would have to memorize everything. She had high expectations from which she never wavered.

9. Don't talk too much. It will make people hate you. Wise people listen much more than they talk. Grandma always reminded me that we have one mouth and two ears for a reason. It is okay to listen and process. Once it's out of your mouth, there is no turning back.

10. People will treat you how you allow them to treat you. Train them from the beginning. People will do only what you allow them to do.

11. I can't help you if you are helping the bear. Even though they are now endangered, bears are known as very versatile animals. They can live in extreme temperature and are omnivores who can eat a variety of different foods to survive. They typically do not need help to do so. What bears are

you allowing to reside in your life?

12. What you learn from school books will get you a job; what you learn from the Bible will make you successful in life. The most important aspects of my grandmother's life was her faith in God and her commitment to prayer. For her, this was not limited to church attendance or religious denomination.

Daily she sought a personal encounter with God and trusted the Lord to guide her steps and her words. Grandma Lena would pray for sometimes hours at a time. I remember hearing her call the names of her children and grandchildren in prayer and know that those prayers are the foundation of the success that we have experienced as a family collectively. Her works were performed privately and she never sought attention or recognition for them.

LaTonya Bolden has been a high school science and mathematics educator for the past seventeen years in North Carolina and Georgia. She has also served as a youth pastor and community advocate in

Harlem, New York. LaTonya and her husband, Arthur, created and manage Bold Minds, a non-profit organization which introduces inner city youth to STEM experiences, outdoor activities, peer group leadership opportunities, and a personal exploration of career, hobby and special interests. LaTonya lives in Atlanta with her husband and adorable dog, Cuddy. She has two beautiful adult daughters, Natasha and Kayla, who reside in Iowa and California. LaTonya is also a member of Delta Sigma Theta Sorority, Incorporated. In her spare time, she enjoys watching documentaries, traveling with family and parasailing around the world. She may be reached at **Latonyabolden1@gmail.com**.

An Anthology Compiled by REGINA "SUNSHINE" ROBINSON

Train people to treat you well from the beginning

CHAPTER SIX
ABUNDANT LOVE

Her Story: *Doshia Rebecca Cowser Miller*

My "grandmother" story is about my great aunt Doshia Rebecca Cowser Miller. She was born February 9, 1894, and died July 16, 1978. She survived some very hard times in the Deep South including segregation and Jim Crow Laws. I can remember her telling me stories about what her life was like as a child. Although she lived her entire life in poverty, she never talked about her life as a tragic tale. She always emphasized the good.

The families were all poor, so people helped each other, shared what they had, and looked out for their neighbors. We called her Aunt Doshia or Momma. She married a man that everyone said was mean as heck. He died before we were born so I never knew her husband, Uncle Edger L. Miller. She never had any children of her own, but she raised her sister's children. Then, she raised us, her sister's grandchildren. Her sister's name was Rena Cowser and she died when my mother was a toddler. My mother and her siblings were raised by Aunt Doshia. Then, she got us when my older sister was three years old and my twin sister and I were six weeks old.

She was about 72 when she took on the responsibility of raising three children aged three and under. I remember her being kind and gentle. She never spanked us or even raised her voice in anger. The only time that I can recall her showing a spark of anger was when the white woman that she was cleaning house for gave my older sister a play broom and told her that she could work for her when she grew up. My Aunt Doshia snapped and told the white woman that my sister would not be working for her. She was mad as heck when she got home and told us that story.

As an adult with children of my own, I am amazed by Aunt Doshia's gentle spirit. I know that it had to be difficult trying to provide for us, but she did it. Country black folks grew their own food and shared meats and vegetables with their neighbors. So we never went without food. In fact, Aunt Doshia was a great cook and we had large feasts every day. There was never a lack of food at our home. She was also very neat and clean. We lived in an old house, but it was so clean and comfortable. Her beds had handmade quilts on them and everything was always nice in our home. Aunt Doshia was so clean that she even had us to sweep the dirt path leading up to the front door steps.

Aunt Doshia was a gift to our lives. Our mother was mentally handicapped and unable to care for us. No one else wanted the responsibility. Aunt Doshia took us in and loved us. She raised us in church and taught us the importance of getting a good education. She had been denied an education as a child. I can remember her marking an 'X' for her signature because she didn't know how to sign her name. But she did learn to read and write before she died. She always encouraged us to do our best in school. Education has always been important to me because it was so important to my Aunt Doshia.

My Lesson

I learned so many lessons growing up with my Aunt Doshia. She raised me and my siblings during the formative years of our lives. She died when I was twelve years old. We were on our own from that point. Her lessons in life and faith in God are what sustained us after she was gone. I remember Aunt Doshia humming Christian spirituals around the house. She had such a deep faith in God and He never let her down. He provided for her and the three little children that she took in. We didn't have a lot, but we always had what we needed. When she ran out of something, she would go to God in prayer and someone would always show up with what we needed. She totally relied on God for her every need.

I think the greatest lesson that Aunt Doshia taught me is that being a Christian is much more than just going to church on Sunday. Being a Christian is about being a servant of the Lord; his hands and feet in the earth. Aunt Doshia displayed Christian character in front of us. One thing that sticks out in my mind is how she would always feed people who came to visit. People loved to visit her because she was such a great cook and they knew that she would feed them.

Well, there was a man with Tuberculosis in the community. No one wanted him in their home because they feared that they would catch TB. Aunt Doshia brought this man into her home, sat him at her table and fed him like a king. She treated him with the same dignity and respect that she showed to the preacher when he came to visit. I was a child, but this love that she showed to the outcast man with TB stayed with me. She was a true child of God, a person who truly trusted God and obeyed what He said in His word.

As a child, I dreamed of the day when I would grow up and be able to take care of my Aunt Doshia. I wanted to give her the world because I felt that she deserved it. She died before I got the opportunity to bless her, but I feel that her spirit lives on in me. I am so much like my Aunt Doshia. My friends tell me that I am such a "caretaker." Just like my Aunt Doshia, I take care of people. I grew up and became a Registered Nurse. Then, I returned to school and got a Masters degree in Education. Just like my Aunt Doshia, I hum Christian songs around the house to help me to get to a place of peace. Just like my Aunt Doshia, I raised my sister's children. My twin sister suffers from epilepsy and needed assistance with raising her children after the divorce from their father. I stepped up and did for my nieces what Aunt Doshia had done for me. I loved them and cared for them.

Aunt Doshia taught me to love God and to love His people without judgment. Her legacy of love is alive and well.

Cescelie Jelks is a loving wife and mother of two teenagers. She is married to her high school sweetheart of 34 years. She is a Registered Nurse with a Master's degree in Education. Cescelie homeschools her children with an emphasis on African American studies and STEM education. Cescelie is currently preparing to launch a nonprofit organization called "Blessed to be a Blessing." The purpose of the nonprofit is to introduce STEM education to underprivileged youth and to help them to attend college debt free. Cescelie's vision for her life is to be a highly sought after author and motivational speaker who travels around the world motivating the masses. To reach Cescelie, email her at cesjelks@gmail.com.

An Anthology Compiled by REGINA "SUNSHINE" ROBINSON

Treat everyone like a King

CHAPTER SEVEN
ROYAL QUEEN

Her Story: *Georgia Glenn*

The lap holds a significant place in my heart.

To lay on the lap of a loved one represents humility, vulnerability, and it's the one place we hold our babies the moment their lives start.

"Baby" was the name my grandmother called me when it was just us two, but what I later found out was grandma had a way of making everyone feel "*baby*" was only the name she affectionately called you.

Laying my head on her lap was a sacred place as I attentively listened to her divine wisdom drawn in by the radiant *behuety* of her sweet heart and face.

My Queen Georgia was the youngest of four sisters; in fact, her eldest sister and my great aunt were named Queen, which isn't really surprising.
I came from a long line of royal queens, including my Grandmother Georgia Glenn.

I remember way back when she showed me she was more than a grandma, but my eldest friend. Unselfishly she gave more than she took, even in her more seasoned years she was so gorgeous she made people take a second look.

But it was her book smarts and ability to write in rhyme that impressed me almost every time. She was my first pen pal when my mother moved us across the states… I still have letters and cards she wrote to date.

My grandma was the chosen person to seek if I wanted good sound advice, and if she didn't agree with you you'd never really know because her truth and voice was still pleasantly nice.

She was the first person I sought when my marriage was going through fire, she then shared how she and my grandfather went through, and how it made them both seek God who was higher.
Her inspiring words are what helped me to grow; she never gave her opinion, but what she knew and know.

It was her confidence I sought, the kind of wise counseling that can't be taught or bought. She had such a peaceful, yet strong soul and it is evident in the lessons she showed how as a black woman to never fold anything but clothes.

She told me how she fought for what she wanted, even her marriage when it was in turmoil. Saying, "Baby, the grass isn't greener, you just gotta plant in good soil."

If not for her love, I don't know what I would've done; God truly broke the mold when he sent this one. Queen Georgia indeed and in deed was heaven sent.

An Anthology Compiled by REGINA "SUNSHINE" ROBINSON

Slow to pass judgment of those who crossed her path; a year passed and my oh my how I miss her adorable humor and laugh.
Never seen her mis-treat others, she dealt with them fair, regardless of hue she lived out the Golden Rule "Treat others as you'd want them to treat you."

Her transparency and truth were something I could rely on since my early youth till I had my own children and was grown - knowing the day soon would come. On 2-06-2017, God called my dear Grandmother Georgia Glenn home.

She earned and was presented with a Silver Shiny Crown, honoring and celebrating her as one of the Queen Mothers of the Church til the day her soul laid down.

If it were not for her soft, gentle eyes & firm lap in which I laid to cry on, I'd be good as gone. So, as I remember the words from her lap she poignantly said, "I'll share them with you in hopes you'll be inspired by the words you've thus far read." GOD is so GOoD that there are two O's in His name!" Thank you, God, for being so good to me and to my Grandma, thank you for sharing your light when you came!

My Lesson: "Blessons"

I learned invaluable lessons I call "blessons" from my grandmother. I learned from her that love is not what one says, but what it does. Grandma taught me to fall in love with a man who initially shows he loves and adores me more. Her reasoning being it's easier for a woman to fall in love first and lose herself. My grandfather literally was smitten over my grandmother, so I assume it worked for them because they were married over 50 years prior to his passing. My grandmother taught me to take everything to the LORD because He had to bear the same crosses we now bear. She shared that love is not without challenges, but to be willing to stand strong during the challenging moments. My grandmother was a praying woman who taught me faith is not without works.

Grandma may have been meek, but wasn't weak. She told me she left, with her three small children, her first husband in the 1950's due to his abusiveness. Her words to me, "I don't care who. Never stay with anyone who abuses you... If a man needs to put his hands on you, he doesn't love or respect himself or you."

Another valued lesson (blesson) I learned was giving of yourself doesn't mean giving all of you to the point of losing self. My grandmother was set against getting married a second time and told me she told the Lord, "If I'm to marry again, you gon' have to bring him directly to my door!" In faith she spoke what she desired, and it literally happened the way she requested it. My grandpa literally stumbled upon her door by coming to the wrong (but right) house for a manicure. He fell in love at first sight, having three more children together.

Finally, what I learned was how to observe and discern. To speak in faith or not at all.

The lessons from my grandmothers' lap were wrapped in the aroma of love, essence of truth, and purity of patience. I sat on her lap as one would have sat at the feet of a queen: eager to be fed like a baby bird words of wisdom. My Queen Georgia's wings have now taken flight.

Isna Tianti is first and foremost a child of The Most High. Secondly, a proud mother of three Behuetiful seeds, an author, multi-talented artist, veteran of the USAF and entrepreneur. Isna Tianti is a two time Published Author, Poet, Spoken Word/Visual Artist, Designer, & Motivational Activist. Isna Tianti has been writing poetry and drawing since the age of five, a print model since the age of nine, and runway model since the age of 19. After losing her mother in 1992 in a motor vehicle accident in which she was the passenger, Isna was later diagnosed with PTSD and suffered with other health maladies. Isna Tianti made it her sole mission to trade in her runway modeling for "role modeling" turning her shame to helping herself first then to help others from her pain. She believe her life was spared to share.

Subsequent to moving to Atlanta and after serving in the Air Force, Isna has appeared as a feature on Hank Stewart's "IT Factor"; was chosen by the late "Great" actor, and author & activist Tommy Ford as the winner to feature at the 2015 Hank Stewarts White Linen Affair. In 2016 Isna Tianti opened up for Dr. Umar Johnson and David Banner twice in 2017, and has been sought to speak to children and adults for conferences and the juvenile courts system. Through her poetry, Isna Tianti shares her truth, love and light for all cultures and hues. Isna Tianti has come to learn that we are born on, with, and for purpose. It is our mandate to find the "blessons" in all our lessons.

An Anthology Compiled by REGINA "SUNSHINE" ROBINSON

Speak in faith or not at all

CHAPTER EIGHT
ABOUT THE BUSINESS OF LOVE

Her Story: Ethel Robertson Partlow

When I think of my grandmother, Mrs. Ethel Robertson Partlow, I remember a short, stout woman who ran her home in such a way that we all knew she meant business. She was born in Modoc, SC, and was one of 18 children. Grandmother was a mother of eight children and she loved them. I remember a woman who would rise long before sunrise to tend her garden, plant flowers, wash and hang out clothes. I remember a hot breakfast that always included homemade biscuits and jelly. This all happened each morning before eight o'clock.

She was one of the hardest working women I have ever known. The interesting thing was she did it all in the home. She was a homemaker in every sense of the word. I lived in the home with her along with my grandfather, my mother, my oldest uncle, my youngest aunt and her son. We all lived harmoniously in the house together until my grandfather passed away, and my uncle and aunt both married and moved out to start their own families. That left my mother and I along with my cousin who decided he did not want to live with his mother and stepfather.

From what I remembered, Grandmother did everything associated with the home, without complaint and while singing hymns. A day for her usually consisted of preparing three meals, washing clothes, hanging those clothes outside on a line, and ironing for the family. During the planting season, there would be gardening, canning, yard work to go along with her daily routine. At the end of each day,

Grandmother retreated to her bedroom to read her Bible and to pray.

Her love of God and her family made it an easy choice for me to make caring for my small family a priority.

My Lesson

Today, it is rare to find many grandmothers who can be home during sick days, snow days, afterschool, spring and summer breaks. Grandmothers are now younger with careers of their own. Fortunately, finding childcare was not an issue for my mother or her sisters, because my Grandmother was always there to care for us. The only time she left the house was for doctor's appointments or to attend church. There were a few times that she travelled out of town to visit her children up north, leaving the care of the home to her daughters. Other than that, she was always there. Being home with her did not mean fun and games. We were not allowed to be in bed pass eight o'clock, which by her standards was laziness. The expectation was to be up fully dressed to start the day. To this day my version of sleeping in is six-thirty or seven o'clock.

An Anthology Compiled by REGINA "SUNSHINE" ROBINSON

As I grew up, Grandmother began giving chores during the day. My job along, with making my bed, was washing dishes, ironing sheets and pillowcases, sweeping the kitchen, dining room and porch. Once a week, Grandmother provided my cousins and I a push broom to sweep and mop the driveway. Yes, you read that right, sweep and mop the driveway!

Grandmother had a no-nonsense approach to discipline. She did not permit playing in the house. There was no running in and out. We did not dare step foot in the living room. She was from the era of You Get Your Own Switch To Be Whipped. There was not a lot that we would get away with. That was the price of having her home and being present. I admit that when I was younger I did not appreciate her approach.

Grandmother was born in 1901, and she was old school. Children were to be seen and not heard. Attempting to engage in grown folk conversations resulted in a quick back hand. Adults were honored and respected. We asked permission to use the telephone while she stood nearby making sure that we asked politely to speak with our friends. Having good manners were taught from an early age. Manners were practiced in the home. Grandmother believed that what you did in the home you would do outside the home. When in public we knew what was expected of us. Her ways seemed over the top at that time, but there was a method to her madness.

The last few years of her life, Grandmother spent bedridden. Family cared for her so that her remaining time could be spent in the comfort of the home she loved. It is going on 22 years without her, and manners are still an important part of our family. That, along with other lessons she instilled in us that I taught my sons, such as, "You are known by the company that you keep." Honestly, I hated when she said that. I was not allowed to associate with just anyone. There were places that I could not go. I appreciate now that I was not allowed to go to the local hangout in our community where many engaged in drinking, smoking, and other risky behavior at an early age. As I got older I understood that character can be misrepresented by associations. These are lessons that I have passed down to my sons and hope that they will pass to their children.

From what I hear, being a grandmother is an awesome experience: you get to spoil your grandbabies, then send them home. When that time comes for me, I look forward to spoiling mine while also teaching them manners, the importance of good character, and kindness. I do not know a lot of what my Grandmother went through in her early years, but I know that it shaped her into a woman who possessed an inner strength that could have only come from her faith in God.

The quality time that was spent with her, whether shelling butter beans, snapping string beans, or just sitting on the porch listening to her sing hymns, I will cherish for a lifetime.

Clarissa Partlow is the creator and writer for the "Finding My Fifty Plus Life" blog. She recently relocated to Smyrna, GA from Greenville, SC, where she has unleashed her passion for writing. Clarissa is a featured columnist with *Bold Plus Magazine*. Clarissa is the mother of two adult sons, Kristofer and Kevon, and has one daughter-in-love Amanda. Clarissa is trusting God as she reimages life as a woman in her fifties. Contact Clarissa on Facebook: @fiftypluslife, via email at finding50plus@gmail.com, and visit her website www.findingmyfiftypluslife.com.

CHAPTER NINE
SACRIFICE IN LOVE

Her Story: Harriet LeCurkis

I did not know my grandmother in the flesh, but because of the wonderful man she raised – my father George – I knew her in spirit. My grandmother was Harriet LeCurkis. I imagine she was an elegant woman, with a warm and caring spirit. I know that she was a hardworking woman committed to excellence, based on some of the things my father shared about her. These are qualities Grandmother Harriet instilled in my father, and he in his children, and for which I am forever grateful.

An Anthology Compiled by REGINA "SUNSHINE" ROBINSON

Grandmother Harriet died of a massive heart attack at the age of 45, long before I was born. I suspect she worked herself into the ground. Grandmother Harriet was born in 1900 and grew up in deeply segregated Jacksonville, Florida. She was beautiful and attracted a lot of male attention – including that from white men. A successful Canadian businessman wooed her and at the age of 17, she gave birth to her only child, my father. Their relationship did not last, yet Grandmother Harriet had a child to raise. She was a companion to a wealthy businesswoman, and made the hard decision to send her only child to live with relatives so that she could work and provide the best life for him which she possibly could.

As a mother myself, I can only imagine the heartache she must have endured, missing my father's first steps, first word, and first time riding a bike. I admire Grandmother Harriet's courage and fortitude, and even her ability to change course when things turned so horribly wrong.

One day Grandmother Harriet went to visit my father during his elementary school years. She did not write ahead as she usually did, she decided to surprise them. Well, the surprise was on her: she arrived to find her son dressed not in the fine clothing she had sent, but rather in a home-spun dress, at the age of nine. Grandmother Harriet was furious! When she confronted her relative, she admitted that they had sold the clothing and used the money to offset their own expenses. Although sympathetic to her plight, Grandmother Harriet could not accept her son wearing a dress for any reason. She packed him up and took him with her, vowing to never part with him again. And she did not until she passed.

I remembered that story as I raised my own children, doing what was necessary to ensure that they stayed with me – no matter what. When my husband and I divorced, my girls were very small – three and five years old. I needed to work, but wanted to be available to them should something happen at school. So, I made the decision to work at night.

It was rough. I am a retired registered nurse, and working at night in a hospital means working HARD. Some of the emergencies we handled still haunt me, and I pray for those families every single day. But it was because of those hospitals being open 24-7-365 that I was able to be there for my girls. I had a sitter stay with them during the night as I worked. When I got home in the morning, I got the girls ready, took them to school, and then came home to sleep. I did this until they were in fourth and fifth grades. It was then that I took a day job because they were old enough to come home and lock the house until I got home a couple of hours later, thus, "latch-key" kids.

When my father married my mother Annie Mae, he had his mother's love forefront in his mind. He knew he wanted as his lifemate a woman who loved her family above all but God, one whose commitment to her children would move mountains. He and my mother were married 51 years, and raised four children including myself. They did what in those days was virtually unheard of: sent four children to college in the 1960's.

It required sacrifice on both of their parts to make it happen. For my father, it meant working multiple jobs, and for my mother it meant becoming a housewife after working so hard to obtain her degree from Bethune Cookman College.

Despite the adjustment in finances, my mother still found the resources to send me and my sister and brothers to piano and voice lessons, encouraged us to participate in sports, and church activities. Although I was not able to be home during the day to greet my children after school, I knew that I could not do less, and provided the piano, dance, gymnastics, and Girl Scout experiences for my girls. When they got older, they participated in the debutant cotillion, high school marching band, church youth group, and NAACP Talent competitions. I attempted to uphold my mother's famous saying: be all you can be; try a little of everything to test your talents to see what you are good at, and see what you like.

And, of course, I must mention that my mother instilled the love of the Lord in us. It is only fitting that I conclude that she always felt that it was her unwavering faith in God, and the love of Jesus in her heart, that allowed her to encourage the development and growth of our family reunion.

Grandmother Harriet and my mother got along well. When my father was drafted into World War II, she came to live with my mother and my older sister, their only child at the time. Grandmother Harriet embraced my mother as the daughter she never had, and my mother embraced Grandmother Harriet as the child who lost her mother at age four. Grandmother Harriet lived with our family until she passed, when my older sister was four.

An Anthology Compiled by REGINA "SUNSHINE" ROBINSON

I am the daughter of this legacy of love, bound together by these wonderful women, who have passed down through the generations, and I strive to do the same.

My Lesson

In summary, I learned from my grandmother to never give up, even when things seem bleak with no hope in sight. I learned that children are a blessing, and they make every trial and sacrifice worth the effort to overcome. And I learned that God is faithful; He gives us everything we need and our deepest heart's desire.

Patience Champion Mitchell is a Senior Editor with the Leading Through Living Community publishing division. She is a retired registered nurse and proud Florida A&M University Rattler. Patience is the daughter of the late Rev. and Mrs. George and Annie Mae Champion, has two adult daughters Lynita Mitchell-Blackwell and Patricia A.

Mitchell, and doting grandmother of Justin and Angelica. Patience loves serving in the community with her church Big Bethel AME and sorority Delta Sigma Theta, reading novels, and traveling.

An Anthology Compiled by REGINA "SUNSHINE" ROBINSON

Love in excellence, and demand the same from your children

CHAPTER TEN
WEAR YOUR FUR...
EVEN IN THE SUMMER

Her Story: Annie Mae Williams Champion

My grandmother Annie Mae Williams Champion was a grand dame. She was a beautiful woman, inside and out – and she knew it. Grandma passed that confidence and self-awareness down to her children and grandchildren. And even when we tried to forget the greatness that resided in us, we were always reminded by the things that were not so little. What were not-so-little things?

Feeling good in spite of what others think.
Being faithful to family and friends, especially during hardship.

Being a witness of God's love for us, even when it was uncomfortable.

Grandma was born in March 4, 1912 in Metcalf, Georgia. Her parents were loving, spirit-filled people who did not allow their humble surroundings to define who they were. Grandma's mother died when she was four years old, so she always felt the void of not having her own mother raise her. Yet, she was blessed with aunts and older cousins who loved and cared for her as if she were their own. Added to that, Grandma had her big sister and best friend forever, Chestina, by her side. It was a blessing the girls had each other, because it was that close bond that brought them through the rough times ahead that included world wars and depressions.

World War I claimed the lives of many of Grandma's friends and some of her cousins.

The Great Depression, which was even greater for black folks, claimed the sanity of even more loved ones.

And yet… Grandma's faith grew even more during those times. She attended Bethune Cookman University (then Dayton-Cookman Collegiate Institute) by picking strawberries and other produce every other semester, saving money to pay her tuition. Grandma had the honor of singing with the Choir, and one of their most memorable performances was before First Lady of the United States of America Eleanor Roosevelt.

She graduated from Bethune Cookman College with her teaching certificate and absolutely LOVED teaching elementary school students. She viewed education as one of the most esteemed fields of study and service, and instilled in her students academic excellence as well as life skills. Grandma taught her students to read and write, and how to set a table. She taught them arithmetic, and how to shake one's hand.

Grandma believed that looking great was a large part of feeling great. Long after she left the classroom to be a full-time homemaker, Grandma continued to teach those around her to BE great. I remember one time during our annual family reunion, one of my older female cousins wanted to wear to church a pair of wrinkled black pants and striped shirt that had seen better days. Grandma took one look at her and said, "You ain't sittin' next to me wearin' dem britches."

The world stopped.

We were stunned. Remember, my grandmother was a lovely, educated woman with beautiful manners. When she started splitting verbs, using slang, and dropping consonants, you knew trouble was around the corner – that train was never late.

Another cousin saw the storm that was about to take us all out, grabbed my pants-clad cousin by the arm, and took her back to her room. In five minutes flat, my cousin came out of that room dressed like she had some sense, i.e., like she was going to the House of the Lord.

Grandma was not the type of person to make fun of someone who could not afford better. If my cousin truly only had that pair of pants and shirt, then of course that is what she would have been welcomed in with open arms. But my cousin DID in fact have better, and that was what had Grandma so angry. As a person who grew up not having much, to raising her own children with lean years that included sometimes celebrating "Santa" after December 25th when things went on sale, my grandmother was no stranger to lack and struggle. But during those hard times, Grandma always said that you don't have to have something new, but it was to be your best, clean and tidy. God blessed us with everything we have, and it was respect and honor to Him that we show up and out the best way we can.

I truly think that was the reason why Grandma always wore her mink, even in the summer. There was this one time the women of the church held their annual day. It was a BIG DEAL: everybody who was anybody in the black community of South Florida Christendom was there. And Grandma wore her pristine white two-piece suit, shoes matched to the hue, huge floral hat… and her fur. In June. In Miami. One of our cousins, about my mom's age, saw Grandma and said in disbelief, "Aunt Mae, is that a mink?!" Grandma looked down her nose (like she was not 5'2" to my cousin's 5'7"), grandly flicked the tail of that fur over her shoulder, turned away, and said with all the regal disdain she could muster, "Yes." And walked away. Man, we laugh about that to this day!

But doing your best and being your best was no laughing matter in our family. During the years my grandmother worked those fields to go to college, her brothers and sisters sent money and aid to help. And when she got on her feet and married my grandfather, Grandma did the same – and sometimes that help meant providing a home for their children, safe harbor by some who were sought by the Klan, and living a life of true love and service with my grandfather George – an AME church pastor - of 51 years that brought people to accept Christ as their Lord and Savior.

As I write this passage thinking of all my grandmother taught me, I realize that there is no way I could ever capture everything. And that is good, because it means that she gave so much that her cup runneth over – and so has mine. Runneth over with love, goodness, and grace.

I love you Grandma.

My Lesson

So what did I learn from my grandmother?
- Do your best and be your best to the best of your ability and circumstances.

- Always give more than what people pay you for and expect of you. Your work is for God's glory, not man's appreciation.
- Love people. They are doing the best they can with what they know they have, and sometimes it's up to you to show them how much more is within them.

Lynita Mitchell-Blackwell is a transformational leadership champion! As the CEO of Leading Through Living Community and BOLD Favor Media Group, she enjoys inspiring, motivating, coaching and propelling people to be successful in the businesses, families, and communities. An attorney, CPA, certified Christian life coach, publisher and member of the Forbes Coaches Council, Lynita is a woman of many achievements and has received several honors across her professions and the communities in which she has lived and served. Lynita is the loving wife of Rev. Brian K. Blackwell and proud mom of Angelica. Contact Lynita at www.LynitaMitchellBlackwell.com.

Lessons from My Grandmother's Lap

CHAPTER ELEVEN
MAMA'S SWEET BREAD

Her Story: Mary Martin Tolbert

My grandmother, Mary Martin Tolbert, was the third of six children of Will (Bud) and Mary Ann Wright Martin. Her parents were born shortly after the abolishment of slavery. When my grandmother, whom we called Mama, was

An Anthology Compiled by REGINA "SUNSHINE" ROBINSON

born in 1913, her father, Bud Martin, was a sharecropper in Troy, SC. They eventually moved to Greenwood, SC.

I grew up in Philadelphia, Pennsylvania, but every summer we would go to Market Street Train Station in route to Greenwood, SC. We always arrived in Greenwood before daybreak and although we were all so tired, we were excited to get to Mama's house. Her house was on the corner of Chapel and Milwee Streets with three rooms, a kitchen, and a small parlor. Until 1968, there was no indoor plumbing and the toilet was outside… yes an outhouse. The outhouse was definitely a trauma that made me happy to return to indoor plumbing. Every morning someone had to dump and wash all of the "pots." Unfortunately, since I was younger than my aunts, and older than the others, it usually was my job. I enjoyed telling my children about outhouses and "pots" when they complained about washing the toilets!

I loved Mama's house. When I was really young, my sisters and I were the only children. Eventually, my cousins came along and every summer that little house hugged four adults and a bunch of children. Some of us slept with our aunts or grandmother, but most of us slept on "pallets" on the floor.

Contrary to what you might think, it was a comfortable pile of blankets, sheets and a pillow. We were normally there during the summer, so it wasn't cold at night.

Those summers were full of fun and adventure. I learned how to cut wood for the wood heating stove and cooking stove. That heating stove made the best cornbread, fried chicken, greens, pinto beans, cakes, pies and anything else Mama decided to cook on it! I remember watching her cook food that was plain, but more delicious than any restaurant.

I also remember watching the adults make soap to wash the dirt from clothes and us. Outside, clothes were boiled to cleanliness. I'm sure I still have scars from boiling cloth falling on my arms and legs.

When I was in the second grade, Mama got really sick. We came to Greenwood during the summer and stayed for an entire year. I was basically homeschooled for the third grade, when home schooling was not a "thing". Mama was very sick, and I was too young to understand what was actually happening. I know now that she was epileptic, which caused seizures. Although she had up and down moments, I am glad she lived for many, many years after that horrendous episode.

Mama was a baker for the public school and other families. We all learned how to bake something from her. My favorite thing she made was "Sweet Bread". I think I'm the only grandchild that remembers sweet bread. Whenever she baked cakes she would make sweet bread, a thin cake without icing. When my mom baked cakes she would always bake the leftover cake batter in a pan for us to munch on. When my children and grandchildren were young, I would do the same thing for them, but it was nothing like Mama's sweet bread. When she was older and retired, she would still bake cakes and pies for the family and sweet bread. Eventually, as dementia began to set in, she no longer remembered sweet bread and I had not asked her for the recipe.

My Lesson

Mama's life, dementia and death taught me three things: learn a skill and perform it to the best of your ability; never refuse to take pictures; and always ask for things you want before the source is irrevocably unavailable.

She only completed the third grade, but she was wiser than anyone I knew. She was an awesome baker and she did it well. I learned to be serious about my career and I tried to pass those lessons to my sons. She hated taking pictures, so there are only a few circulating among us. We now take many family pictures so that generations to come will have a face to go with the stories. I have two pictures of Mama, and neither depicts her the way I remember. I tell my children about her so they can at least imagine her through my stories.

Because we all grew up together in that little house on Chapel Street, we are a very close family. We learned how important a relationship with God is for our family. Mama started a tradition back in the '70's that we have continued to this day: Tolbert Family Thanksgiving Weekend. It is an awesome time for us to cook good food and catch up with each other. When we were younger, grown-ups cooked and we helped. When they thought we were ready, we took over the event planning. Now we have turned it over to the next generation. Hopefully, this tradition will continue for generations to come. I created an email group and a Facebook group entitled "Mary Tolbert's Grandchildren" which helps us to keep in touch with each other throughout the year.

An Anthology Compiled by REGINA "SUNSHINE" ROBINSON

Mary Martin Tolbert taught us something that cannot be found in schoolbooks: God is more important than anything. If you think money and property are the basis for a legacy, you are sadly mistaken. Family is the most important commodity anyone can own. She taught us that no matter how poor or rich we are, we are one family, and we take care of our seniors and each other. We have tried to live up to her legacy.

Oh, by the way, when I was 30-ish, I realized Sweet Bread was the leftover batter from her cakes. Ha! Go Figure… Nevertheless, no one makes Sweet Bread like Mama.

Dr. AudreyAnn Moses is a Certified Christian Life Coach and Mental Wellness Counselor. She is involved in several community-based programs focusing on personal and professional development. Dr.

Moses taught psychology and has written several articles and conducted workshops on personal growth and transition. She has written three novels: *Saved By Grace…*; *Uninvited Memories* and *The Swing*, which can be found on Amazon or by contacting her directly. AudreyAnn and husband, Leonard, currently live in the quaint rural community of Cokesbury in Hodges, SC. They have four adult children, ten grandchildren and one great-grandson which AudreyAnn feels qualifies her to write stories of Christian family dysfunction, love and devotion to each other and to God.

An Anthology Compiled by REGINA "SUNSHINE" ROBINSON

Learn a skill and perform it to the best of your ability

Lessons from My Grandmother's Lap

CHAPTER TWELVE
MY PERSONAL VESSELS OF AGAPE LOVE

Their Story: Maebelle Dardy and Mary Mincey

An Anthology Compiled by REGINA "SUNSHINE" ROBINSON

The most anticipated day in the history of kindergarten was coming up in a week and I could barely contain my excitement. I was finally going to get a chance to show off my most prized *"possessions"* during Show and Tell: my great and great-great grandmothers! Yes, I know, it isn't very often that you hear a five-year-old referring to her grannies as "prized *possessions*". But if you know anything about me, you'd know that I was extremely possessive and proud of them both. I was so proud watching the other kids enjoy them as much as I did as they told funny stories about growing up on a farm. They were my very own vessels of love, laughter, patience, peace, safety, teaching, and preaching. The agape love lessons that my great-grandmother Maebelle and great-great grandmother Mary shared from their lips transcends time and human understanding.

On the first day of kindergarten you'd think that they were sending me to kiddie *Sing Sing*. My mom was inconsolable, *my* Gramma refused to stay at home even though she was ill, and *my* Mah-Mah asked the teacher if they could stay for half of the day (the answer was *no*). You see, my grannies were children hoarders. They absolutely loved their children and wanted to enjoy them forever. Though my mom worked at a family owned daycare, it was understood that I was to stay at home for as long as possible. They even persuaded my aunt and uncle to remove my cousin from [her aunt's] daycare! Our days were filled with good cookin', learning, singing, bible study, and laughter. Our favorite time at the "Granny Preschool of Love" was music/recess. They'd sing *"Run, Don't Look Back"* seemingly forever, while my cousin and I would run in place as fast as we could. They laughed more than they sang, and we laughed more than we ran. I felt... enjoyed, and that our words and very existence were more valuable than gold. My grannies listened to me as if I were a master orator, hanging on to every word and enjoying every lilt.

My Gramma Mary was born in 1896, in rural Georgia. She spoke with the wisdom of a bible scholar and the passion of a freedom fighter. She and my Mah-Mah were mother-daughter relationship goals (as the young folks say), as their hearts were intertwined, beating synchronously. My Mah-Mah Maebelle moved to Miami, FL from Dublin, GA, with her husband and three children in 1944, at the age of 23. After some years of city life, her husband left, and she was left to raise 5 children on her own. Once word got back to Mah-Mah Maebelle's mother Mary, she (Mary) set out to

Miami the next day. My Gramma helped my Mah-Mah raise her children, as well as two more generations after them. They laughed and showed more love than anyone I've ever known, regardless of heartbreak and pain they experienced.

Several weeks after my Gramma passed in 1988, *my* Mah-Mah and my mom packed up our house. We moved out on my eighth birthday.

"Mah-Mah, where are we going?" I asked.

"I don't know baby." But she said it with confidence, so I felt confident, too.

That last night in our home, my Mah-Mah prayed in a voice that I had never heard, in a way that was almost foreign to me. It was the most fervent and powerful prayer I had ever heard in my short life. I've tried to put it in words for almost 30 years, and still find it impossible to do so.

My Mah-Mah was very easy-going and slow to anger. Some people tried to take advantage of that and would disrespect her. She'd just say, "True love and forgiveness means looking past their fault and seeing their need," or "Don't be mad at them, pray for them because they're sin sick and don't even know it." The sentiment was admirable, but I just wanted to hit them on top of the head for messing with *my* Mah-Mah! She was my very best friend and favorite human. She was my peace, comfort, safety, conscience, cheerleader, inner voice, and favorite "bunk buddy". I never missed an opportunity to sleep in *my* Mah-Mah's bed. It's as if it absorbed all my fears, uncertainty, and anxiety. I would even get out of my bed in the middle of the night as a grown woman, drive to her house just to get in her bed!

My Lessons

These two beautiful and powerful vessels were the first bible I've ever read. Their lives provided me with my first lessons of love, faith, and belief. Because of their walk, I knew that one day I had to give my life to Christ as I had the privilege of witnessing the work of God working inside and manifesting on the outside. Though my story isn't all rainbows and sunny days, I'm thankful that I was taught how to pray. Gramma taught me to speak up when wrong is wrong, no matter who's the culprit. She would often say, "Right is right, wrong is wrong, and the twain will never meet."
My greatest lesson from *my* Gramma is knowing that standing on God's word will always elevate you

above everything and everyone leaning to their own understanding.

God saw fit to bless me with *my* Mah-Mah for thirty years on this earth. We were inseparable for most of that time. Most of what I learned from her can't be translated or even transliterated. She taught me how to exercise my gift of prophesy, to not be afraid of what I do not understand. Her prayers live in me; I can still feel them. I'm sure that I am still here because of them. She taught me how to forgive, and let go of pain so deep I know it was meant to destroy me. I learned the power of temperance and patience. Loving people the way God wants us to is impossible in the flesh. Learning to love in the Spirit was my most valuable lesson.

Melissa D. McMillan, a self-professed "grandma's baby" moved to Warner Robins, GA in 2006, in pursuit of a peaceful place to start a career (and be closer to her great-grandmother). While working her way through graduate school to

complete her goal of becoming a Physical Therapist, the Florida Agricultural and Mechanical University graduate realized that her passion was teaching and mentoring young people. God called, Melissa answered, and now the wife and mother is embarking on her journey to becoming a voice for the voiceless. She's stepping out on faith and standing in her purpose with the birth of her Imperial Youth with Purpose ministry: a safe and grace-filled space for young people to speak freely about sexual abuse and begin the process of giving the shame back to its origin and healing.

An Anthology Compiled by REGINA "SUNSHINE" ROBINSON

Right is right, wrong is wrong, and the twain will never meet

Lessons from My Grandmother's Lap

GRANDMA

GrandMa a woman of extreme strength, courage, and LOVE;

Beautiful WOMAN, virtuous, gentle, and now at peace and free as a dove.

GrandMa, someone on who our admiration was built around;

An Anthology Compiled by REGINA "SUNSHINE" ROBINSON

For her DEDICATED servant's heart, as a wife, mother, sister, grandmother, friend on this earthly ground.

GrandMa, we will forever hold in our hearts, your perseverance and sacrificial LIFE as a wonderful mother to our mothers and fathers;

We have gained wisdom in raising your great-grandsons and great-granddaughters.

GrandMa, we will always RESPECT all that you endured till the end,

You fought the good fight of FAITH with GOD because you knew with HIM, you would WIN.

GrandMa, as you enter your heavenly home, May you rest in peace for that is what you truly DESERVE;

You will be missed and remembered for your self-less Love and Honor in which we will PRESERVE.

GrandMa
By Shaquita Maxey

Dear Reader,

I pray the stories on these pages have blessed you. I hope you felt the love and were moved to revisit your personal memories. If you feel inspired, write a story about your grandmother. If you weren't fortunate enough to have the kind of grandmother that we did, I pray you are inspired to love others the way you wish you had been loved.

And finally, I hope you dream. Dream about her. Dream about you. Dream about what's next. Because what I know for sure is that my Grandma Snook was most concerned about what was next for me and making sure my dreams came true. So I dream for her and for all the dreams she didn't achieve. I dream for all the sacrifices she made for me to dream. And I dream of the day when I will once again see her face.

My hope is that I make her proud, and all though I miss her, I still rejoice in her "Well Done."

Be Blessed. Keep Winning.

Regina Sunshine

ABOUT THE ORGANIZER

Regina Sunshine Robinson is an Author, Motivational Speaker, Talk Show Host, Empowerment Coach, Corporate Trainer, and Teacher. She is CEO of Regina Sunshine Global Network, parent company to everything Regina Sunshine including EWATE, a Women's Empowerment Organization whose main purpose is to empower and encourage women to be all they were created to be in order to fulfill God's perfect plan for their lives. Their slogan is "We'll Help You Get Your SASSY Back." Tune in to Regina's acclaimed talk show "The Regina Sunshine Show" on Comcast 24 People TV Tuesdays at 12 pm EST and on Regina Sunshine Global Network Mondays at 7 pm EST to get a weekly dose of her Regina Sunshine State of Mind. Regina Sunshine is also the Editor in Chief of BOLD Plus Magazine. Regina's personal motto is "It's Not Over Til I Win" and she wins when she sees others "WINNING". For more information, to book her or to follow her on Social Media, go to ReginaSunshine.com

www.ingramcontent.com/pod-product-compliance
Lightning Source LLC
Chambersburg PA
CBHW070512090426
42735CB00012B/2750